THE EARLIEST AMERICANS

By the same author

THE MOUND BUILDERS

THE CAVE HUNTERS

ANCIENT ELEPHANTS

PREHISTORIC MAN AND THE PRIMATES

THE FIRST MAMMALS

PREHISTORIC ANIMALS

THE
Earliest Americans

Written and illustrated by

WILLIAM E. SCHEELE
Director, Natural Science Museum of Cleveland

80394

THE WORLD PUBLISHING COMPANY

CLEVELAND AND NEW YORK

Published by The World Publishing Company
2231 West 110th Street, Cleveland 2, Ohio

Published simultaneously in Canada by
Nelson, Foster & Scott Ltd.

Library of Congress Catalog Card Number: 63–8913

WP

THE EARLIEST AMERICANS

WHO WERE the first Americans? In spite of many years of searching, the answer to that intriguing question is still pretty much of a mystery. Our only clues to the earliest people to occupy this continent are a few flint tools, charcoal, and the bones of animals that have been extinct for twenty-five thousand years or more. This is not very much to go on, but some scientists working in the field are convinced that the earliest Americans did not at all resemble the red-skinned people whom Columbus called Indians.

In the 1920s, archaeologists could trace the ancestry of the American Indians from an Archaic phase of four thousand years ago through an evolution as hunters to settled farmers and traders. Not all of the details of this progress were clear, but no one suspected that there might have been more an-

[7]

cient people on this continent. Had anyone seriously suggested that man was present in North America as the glaciers were melting away ten thousand years ago, the theory would have been laughed off as impossible.

But in 1926 came a turning point in North American archaeology—a discovery which provided the first concrete evidence that man was living on this continent at the close of the great ice age. It came about because a few staff members at the Denver Natural History Museum had become excited at the possibility of finding man-made tools among the bones of animals known to be extinct for many thousands of years.

Two years earlier, such a discovery had been made near Lone Wolf Creek, Texas, on one of the Denver Museum's own fossil-hunting expeditions. Two chipped flint points were found with the bones of a bison known to have been extinct for ten thousand years. But, unfortunately, the field party at the site failed to preserve the evidence of this unusual association.

In 1926, the Denver fossil hunters were about to excavate another promising bone deposit at Folsom, New Mexico. The men left with explicit in-

[8]

structions to watch for any sign of man-made tools among the bones they were investigating. These men had good luck—two broken flint spear points were found in the early stages of digging.

A few days later, a fragment of chipped flint was discovered in a clay layer that also contained ancient bison bones. A block of this earth, containing the bones, was taken up as a chunk and sent to Denver for careful cleaning in the laboratory. To everyone's amazement, the piece of flint proved to be part of a spear point, and the piece matched perfectly with one of the broken blades found early in the digging. Here was good evidence: a blade broken when killing a bison, part of it still resting near the animal's bones.

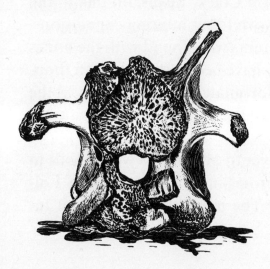

A bison vertebra with a broken flint spear point still in place

This news was circulated as exciting proof of man's great age in the New World. But excitement and optimism were quickly squelched by general doubt of the find among anthropologists and archaeologists.

In 1927, work was continued at the Folsom deposit. Very quickly, more flint points and bison bones were found. When the first piece of chipped flint was observed, all work was ordered to stop before it was uncovered.

A dramatic step was taken at this point. It seemed necessary to establish the accuracy of the museum's find. Telegrams were sent to a number of leading institutions specializing in studies of fossils and prehistoric man. These organizations were asked to send representatives to see the bones and flint pieces before they were fully uncovered.

First to arrive was the famous fossil hunter, Dr. Barnum Brown, from New York City's American Museum of Natural History. Dr. Brown joined Jesse Figgins, the director of the Denver Museum, and several of the museum's trustees in exposing an unusual flint spear point lying between the ribs of an extinct form of bison. Within hours, a second specialist arrived from Washington, D. C., and within a few days scholars arrived from other sections of the country. Later, when these men left Folsom, they were convinced of the significance of the find.

The historic piece of earth containing the bison ribs and flint point was removed and is still displayed in the Denver Museum. The animal is now officially called Figgins' Bison.

The Folsom site had been near a water hole, and since signs of butchering and pond-edge vegetation were abundant, we know that the site itself had been a hunters' camp. Deep layers of soil covering the bones and flint tools had preserved proof of the age of this discovery. Careful comparison with similar soil layers of known age verified the fact that the Folsom site was older than any previously described Indian culture.

Carefully as this important event had been handled, its significance was still questioned by some who had not been present at the site. But a note of caution had been heard, and all those who were engaged in searching for signs of early human beings or the bones of ice-age animals in North America realized that there were new possibilities in their work. When unusual flint objects were found they

The turning point in American prehistoric studies: the ribs of Figgins' Bison and a Folsom point preserved and displayed just as they were found in 1926

demanded new respect, for almost overnight anything had become possible. No one could afford to brush aside the slightest evidence that the works of man and the bones of mammals long extinct might belong together.

[12]

Perhaps the greatest value of the Folsom site was that it destroyed the belief that all of the important discoveries concerning early man in America had been made by 1926. Most scientists at that time were convinced that the American Indians, who came to this continent after the last of the great continental glaciers had disappeared, were the oldest Americans. The possibility that human beings lived in North America more than four thousand years ago had seldom been seriously considered.

The story of man on each of the world's continents varies a great deal. In the United States, those interested in studying the American Indians categorize them into three large groups. The first of these are the living Indians of today and their immediate ancestors who greeted the first European settlers. The more distant ancestors of these same people comprise the second group: the Indians whose mounds and village sites were discovered largely by accident when colonists first farmed the land. The third group are the Paleo-Indians, a term applied to those ancient wandering hunters of whom we first became aware at Folsom, New Mexico, in 1926. It was then that scientists first proved man's existence in America while ice-age mammals were also a part of the scene.

From the moment they were encountered, the American Indians were great curiosities to the rest of the world. European explorers of North America found this stone-age population spread over the entire continent. The origin of these natives was and still is eagerly debated, and objects they used or wore for ceremony, war, or daily living were widely collected.

For a time, the living Indians of the New World held the interest of scholars. But as time passed and settlers uncovered relics buried in their land, men realized that still other Indians had lived here long before the time of Columbus.

Many attempts were made to interpret the early history of the American Indians, and large collections of unusual examples of their workmanship were assembled. Unfortunately for us today, few early collectors recorded the circumstances of their discoveries, and the eager diggers paid no attention to the layers of soil they dug through. Only the perfect or extraordinary pieces were kept. Many things that would have made the story more complete—broken bits of charcoal, flint flakes, broken scraps of tools, even some human or animal bones—were merely observed quickly and then discarded.

There was so much evidence of these people available, however, that piecing together the story of their way of life became the challenge that helped organize the entire science of archaeology. It was clear from the relics preserved that these Indians were not wandering hunters, but farmers who lived in one place the year round, harvested crops, and stored them for winter use. In some cases, trading between tribes or lavish burial rituals were distinctive. House styles could be recognized, tool making was an organized craft, pottery could be classified, and the entire sequence of Indian activities in a single area could be traced for hundreds of years.

Historians and scientists of the late nineteenth and early twentieth centuries continued to find the background of the Indians a challenge. As each fact was put in place an order developed, and there was general agreement that the Indians had arrived on the North American continent some time after the last of the ice-age glaciers had melted away to the northeast. The oldest Indian cultures were assumed to be not more than four thousand years old.

But in the existing records of some old collections there were curious facts that did not agree with this age estimate for the earliest culture in North America. For example, in 1838 and 1839 strange flint points, charcoal, and bones of extinct ice-age mammals had been found together in a Missouri excavation. In 1846, at Natchez, Mississippi, half of a human pelvis and the bones of extinct animals were taken from the same soil layer. Between 1872 and 1879, gravel beds at Trenton, New Jersey, were found to contain human bones, flint points, and the bones of ice-age mammals. These sites and many more held clues to the great antiquity of man in North America.

Had these discoveries been recognized for what they were or had they been explored with methods used today, our knowledge of the Indians' ancestors would present a clearer picture of the past. But in 1890, or even as late as 1925, no one would have dared to suggest that nomadic hunters had lived in portions of this land many thousands of years before the oldest-known Indian culture.

Not until the Folsom excavation in 1926 could concrete evidence of Americans in the ice age be studied by modern archaeological techniques.

Today, fresh sites are excavated by methods that produce uniform and reliable results. Archaeology

A well-managed excavation. Changes of soil layers and signs of man's presence are carefully revealed and then recorded as the digging proceeds

and anthropology have become precise sciences. Similar relics found in different sites can be compared to help determine the age of objects and the soils from which they come.

One of the most useful archaeological dating methods is the process of measuring the radioactive carbon all living plants and animals absorb. When an organism dies, this carbon disintegrates, or decays, at a known rate. In 5,600 years, half of the original carbon 14 will be left. The passage of time since the death of the animal or plant can be calculated by measuring the amount of carbon still present in the remains. This dating method is most accurate for comparatively recent materials and is ideal for the study of the Paleo-Indians.

In 1928, Folsom was again the scene of a major excavation. This time, two digging teams were used: One worked at the bone deposit and the other explored the near-by countryside for signs of camp sites of the hunters who had killed the bison. No evidence of a hunters' camp was discovered, but the crew digging at the bone deposit had better luck. More animal bones were found, and with them were additional spear points, a flint scraper, and an assortment of crude knives.

Though the 1928 effort did not produce startling new facts about the early hunters, it did succeed in convincing skeptics that a very ancient predecessor of the American Indian had hunted and killed a species of bison which had been extinct for at least ten thousand years.

At this point, many people quickly assumed that the earliest Americans had been identified by the spear points found at Folsom, New Mexico.

[18]

Figgins' Bison was a numerous species, larger than the modern bison. The animal ranged over a vast area and was hunted by many prehistoric Americans

It has been the practice to identify past cultures by the names of sites where evidence of their presence was first discovered. This is particularly true when the signs are distinctive and seem to indicate a specialized way of life within a limited area. The name *Folsom man* is a typical example of this practice. But until anatomists are able to agree about

[19]

A bison drive. Primitive peoples of all times used this device to secure meat and skins. Here, the herd is driven over the cliff edge into a log corral by men waving hides

the relationships between the American Indians and their predecessors, most writers prefer to use the term *Paleo-Indian* when referring to all of the big-game hunters who thrived on this continent before the oldest of the red-skinned Indians who were the ancestors of modern tribesmen.

[20]

There is a similar problem of definition concerning the flint spear points used by ancient hunting groups. The process of fluting a blade was quite varied and the practice spanned a long period of time. Rather than try to apply a separate name for each blade variation, the term *fluted point* is used for all blades having any portion of the distinctive "fluted" channel. The name *Folsom* is only applied, however, to the unique spear points first identified at the Folsom site.

Though the fluted points found at Folsom are unique in the prehistoric world, they are not the oldest known from the Western Hemisphere. They are merely one indication of a long and complicated spread of hunting tribes throughout the length and breadth of two large continents.

Those who classify and describe primitive people group them according to the style and variety of objects they created: tools, weapons, utensils, dwellings, methods of food gathering. These and many other facts provide knowledge of how people lived. Soil layers, soil analysis, tree rings, pollen grains, carbon-14 dates, and the proper identification of animal bones provide clues to the age of the sites and the cultures being studied.

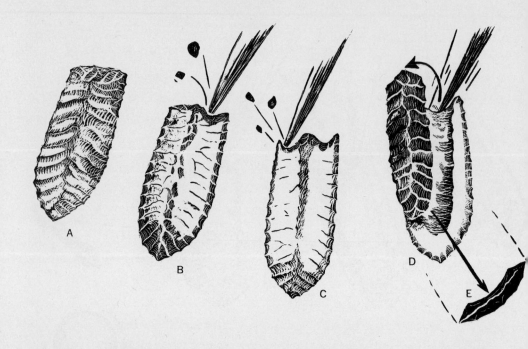

How a fluted point is made. There are many variations of this delicate flaking process

A. *The point roughed out to general form*
B. *Chipping a notch in the base*
C. *Finishing the notch; leaving a striking platform in the middle*
D. *A sharp blow delivered against the striking platform snaps out a long flake, creating one fluted face*
E. *Cross section of the point showing this fluted face*

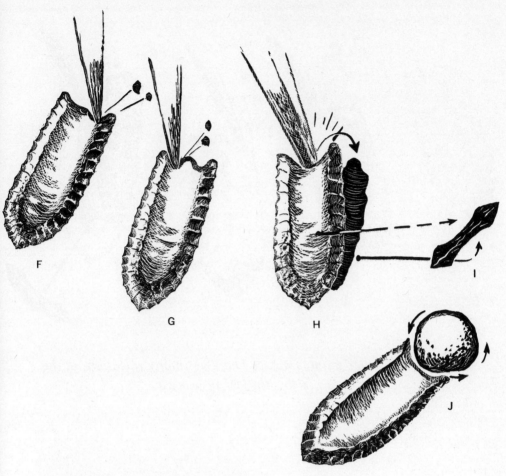

F. *Starting a second basal notch*
G. *Completed basal notch with a striking platform*
H. *A blow against the striking platform removes the second long flake, creating another fluted surface*
I. *Cross section of point showing both fluted faces*
J. *Grinding the base to smooth it; the "ears" and edge have been retouched by fine chipping to sharpen the blade*

Poised to throw. Details of feathers, grip, or design of the throwing stick vary among primitive peoples, but the weapon itself was widely known

When archaeology was a new science, crude arrowheads were assumed to be older than well-made points. It could be demonstrated that crude pottery-making techniques steadily improved and that crude baskets were older than those of beautiful tight weave. All technical and social progress seemed marked by steady improvements in the ways man met his needs.

The classifiers of American Indians were surprised when Folsom spear points turned out to be older than the flint work of any other American native. Here were beautiful blades made by a tech-

[24]

By using a throwing stick to propel a spear or dart, a man can increase the range, speed, and accuracy of his throw. This process, widely used long before the bow became popular, is still used today among some primitive people

nique that required unusual skill and control of flake removal. And since Folsom, other very old flint points of great technical perfection and beauty have been linked with other early hunters. The long-standing idea that ancient man used only crude tools had to be discarded along with the belief that the oldest Americans were recent arrivals on this continent.

After Folsom, ten years passed before another major site was excavated which might reveal more about the hunters of Figgins' Bison. Such a place was known during those ten years by Judge C. C. Coffin and his son, of Fort Collins, Colorado. These men recognized that the flint points they were finding on William Lindenmeier's land were quite different from other local Indian artifacts.

An article about the Folsom exploration in a national magazine led to an exchange of letters that brought representatives of the Smithsonian Institution in Washington, D. C., to look at the Lindenmeier deposit. As a result, extensive digging in the northeastern corner of Colorado was carried on from 1934 to 1938.

The Coffins had found their specimens on the earth's surface, but the major Smithsonian excava-

A distant view of the Lindenmeier site showing sparse vegetation and eroded landscape

tion was located some distance from that spot on the edge of a gully. The party uncovered a prehistoric hunters' camp well buried under soil washed from higher land near-by.

Most of the mammal bones found in this dig came from what appears to have been a heap of butchering refuse tossed along the edge of a small lake or water hole. Nearly all of the bones had been

[27]

crushed or broken, but teeth and the larger pieces were enough to identify the primary quarry of these hunters as the same animal that had been found at Folsom—Figgins' Bison.

There were bones of other animals too, including those of the camel, wolf, fox, and rabbit. Lindenmeier is the only known Folsom site to contain rare camel bones. At the level of the main discoveries, but some distance away, the excavators also found a weathering mammoth tusk which might have been part of the camp debris.

Many styles of knives, scrapers, choppers, and hammers were found at the Lindenmeier site. These had been used to prepare hides, smash bones, and to cut up large meat chunks that had been roughly butchered farther away.

A number of stones were found which seem to have been used to smooth and soften hides. Others were hammers used to flake flint or smash bones. Some fragments look as though they had been used to smooth wooden spear shafts. Hematite fragments were found that had been ground to produce red pigment. One piece of sandstone had a shallow depression in it that was tinged with this red paint. Since sandstone does not occur naturally near the

[28]

side scraper

working edge

snub-nosed scraper

graver

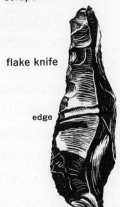

flake knife

edge

carved bone disc

incised

sandstone grinding tool

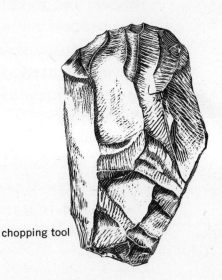

chopping tool

*Artifacts from the Lindenmeier site are typical
of many other sites as well*

site, these crude rock chunks had been carried into the camp as valuable tools.

Some bone fragments from the Lindenmeier ranch show signs of use as chopping or pounding tools. One of the most interesting discoveries made there, however, was three bone disks that had been shaped and crudely decorated. These may have been part of a game or gambling pastime. But most important is the fact that, in this red paint and bone decoration, a glimmer of culture was seen.

The Lindenmeier site also provided the first examples of the methods used to create the fluted points first discovered at Folsom. Spearheads showing work in progress were found, illustrating all steps of manufacture.

Lindenmeier was reopened in 1960 to obtain charcoal that could be processed for an accurate carbon-14 date. Results of the testing provided a

Face of an imaginary beast created from the sacrum of an extinct species of llama, found at Tequixquiac, Mexico. Drilled nostrils and rough-shaped bone edges mark this as one of the very earliest art forms found anywhere in North America

minimum date of 10,480 years, give or take 375 years, and a maximum date of 11,080 years, with the same margin of possible error. This is the oldest of the Folsom sites that have been assigned a date.

Between the time of the Folsom and Lindenmeier explorations, there were many significant finds made throughout this country. Equally vital new sites are still being located today. Some of these explorations have added new animal names and styles of flint points to the growing list of facts about early man in America.

In 1936, New Mexico again became the scene of an important discovery. Five obscure caves in a cliff at the foot of the Sandia Mountains were involved. Of these, the largest became the center of attention.

A student found the caves, and from the dusty floor level of the largest one he recovered an interesting assortment of Indian artifacts. The young man showed these scraps to Dr. Frank Hibben, professor of archaeology at the University of New Mexico. Dr. Hibben knew instantly that any cave containing such evidence should be looked at promptly.

Hibben led an exploring party into the cave and

[31]

had unusually good luck. Almost immediately, the men found bones of a ground sloth, a lumbering giant of the ice age. Their first hope was to discover a relationship between these remains and any human skeletons that might be present, but first there was much work to be done in clearing the mouth of the cave.

This job in itself was fascinating and vital to eventual success, for the accumulation of rubbish, soil, and rocks told its own story of time lapse and climate change. Dust was up to six feet deep; In-

The ground sloth was common in both North and South America during the ice age. Bones of the animal have been linked with evidence of early man on both continents

dian artifacts several centuries old were plentiful, along with bat dung, pack-rat nests, and other debris several thousand years old.

Below the scrambled recent level was a hardened seal of water-borne minerals from one to six inches thick. This layer was the key to the cave's importance; it had been formed during late glacial times as the result of a very wet climate. The layer sealed off lower soil levels and prevented any mixture of materials that might have occurred there.

When this stony crust was removed, the earth beneath was found to be lightly cemented together by minerals. This lumpy near-solid mass was filled with broken bones and the unique spear points that represented Folsom man. The cave at this point was a great success, the first to show that these early Americans were also cave dwellers if a cave were available. Previous discoveries had suggested that these hardy people always lived out in open country.

But there was more to come from Sandia cave. Below the hardened soil containing the Folsom relics was a layer of empty soil, a fine-grained yellow ochre that had been laid down in thin layers by water. The ochre represented a wet climate of several

[33]

thousand years, and it served as another sealer for still lower layers of soil.

Artifacts were found below that seal of ochre. Along with flint points, there were two charcoal hearths, one ringed by small boulders, and splintered animal bones of many kinds. The bones and teeth were from the same list of animal species killed by Folsom people, but the flint spear tips were made in a style new to archaeologists.

These "Sandia" points were rougher than Folsom blades, and they were further distinguished by having a slight "shoulder" chipped into one side near the base. Two other similar forms of points were found in the cave, along with scrapers, flake blades, and two peculiar bone points for projectiles.

The soil layers excavated at Sandia suggested a date for the lowest levels of approximately twenty thousand years. With such clear and indisputable evidence of a culture older than Folsom at hand, there could be no doubt this site was one of the great ones. None the less, it was difficult to fix a date for the contents. The cave had protected the soil layers it held, but outside there were no comparable deposits. They had been altered beyond recognition by erosion and time.

[34]

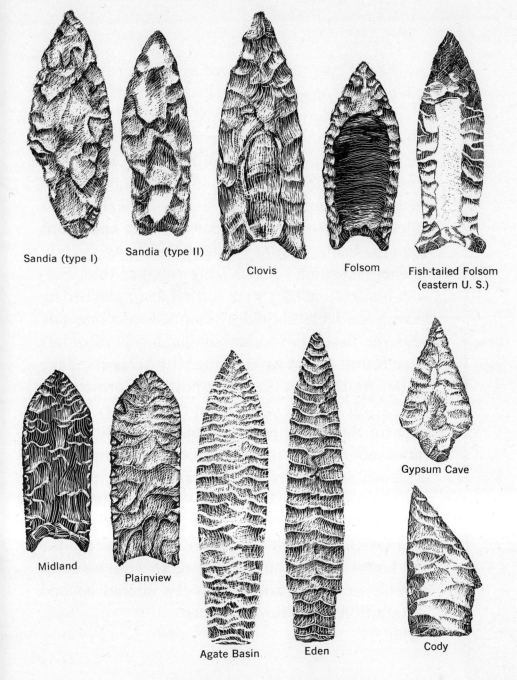

Sandia (type I) Sandia (type II)

Clovis Folsom Fish-tailed Folsom (eastern U. S.)

Midland Plainview

Agate Basin Eden

Gypsum Cave

Cody

*A selection of important flint points
used by prehistoric Americans*

A cave and rock shelter in the American Southwest. Protected locations like this preserve the best record of primitive man throughout the world

It was clear from the dark color of the lowest soil layers in the cave that these deposits represented a wet climate. The upper layers were an accumulation from drier centuries which came after the disappearance of ice-age glaciers.

With such important evidence at hand, a mere

estimated date for Sandia was not enough. Samples had to be submitted for a carbon-14 analysis. One report on an ivory sample from the cave produced a date well in excess of twenty thousand years. Dr. Hibben describes the Sandia cave men as being twenty-six thousand years old.

Could this be the earliest American? Probably not, for it would take a long time for a wandering band of hunters to reach New Mexico from any distant point on the continent. And we can only guess how long it took men to travel on foot from Siberia through Alaska, Canada, and inland on our continent.

But the people of Sandia represent still another

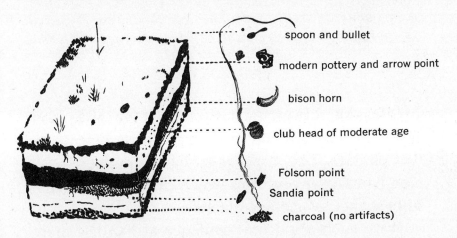

spoon and bullet

modern pottery and arrow point

bison horn

club head of moderate age

Folsom point

Sandia point

charcoal (no artifacts)

A representative sequence of soil layers in the earth containing progressively older signs of man's presence in that area

kind of mystery. The unique flint spear points they made are rare. Some similar points found in other parts of this country have come from the Mississippi River valley and the eastern United States. The only other flint points like them are ones that have been found in France and North Africa. Called Solutrean points, they have a well-established age of forty thousand years.

These facts have led a few men to believe that a crossing from Europe to North America was once possible by way of Iceland, Greenland, and Canada. This is not a widely accepted idea, for the crossing would require an unlikely combination of low water, vast ice sheets, and some form of water transportation. Additional evidence to give weight to this theory, however, is the discovery in the eastern United States of crude stone choppers which resemble early hand tools from Europe.

Crude pebble tools and choppers have been discussed and disputed in America since 1880, but there is little evidence of their age. The best argument in favor of great age is their incredible similarity to European examples that are twenty-five thousand years old. To some archaeologists it is equally incredible that Sandia- and Solutrean-style

[38]

points could have developed independently in two regions so widely separated as France and New Mexico.

Almost every anthropologist agrees, though, that a land bridge once connected Asia and Alaska, and that the first Americans migrated across this dry-land route. The bridge was formed in this way.

During each of the four long periods when the great glaciers of the ice age grew and moved over the land, they accumulated vast amounts of ocean water. This occurred when evaporating sea water was converted to snow or rain, and was then carried to those places where glaciers were forming.

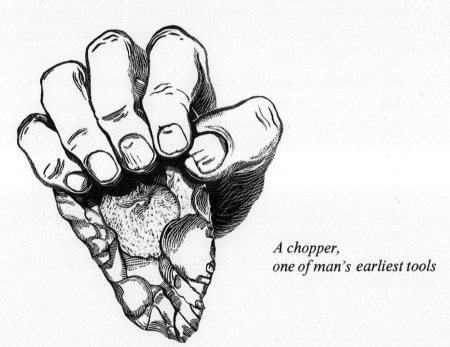

A chopper,
one of man's earliest tools

Men who study glaciers tell us that this process removed enough water from the oceans around the world to lower the sea level at least 300 feet, and more in some areas. Lowering ocean depths a mere 150 feet between Alaska and Asia would connect the two land masses by a broad land bridge. We cannot tell exactly how broad it was, how high above water level, or how long it remained dry; but it is clear that men and animals used that land bridge many times, and that the travelers moved in both directions.

Ocean water was frozen solid in glaciers for hundreds and sometimes thousands of years before it melted back to water. By accepting this view, one can see that there was time enough for the Asia-Alaska land bridge to dry, for grass and trees to grow, and for people to hunt and camp where the ocean now drowns the land, covering what evidence of those events the soil may contain.

Even near the great glaciers life was quite possible. The barren heart of any glacier-covered area would be impassably rough and cold, but rich soil at the edges of the ice fields could nourish animal and plant life. When the ice was moving slowly or stopped for a decade or two, an entire forest could

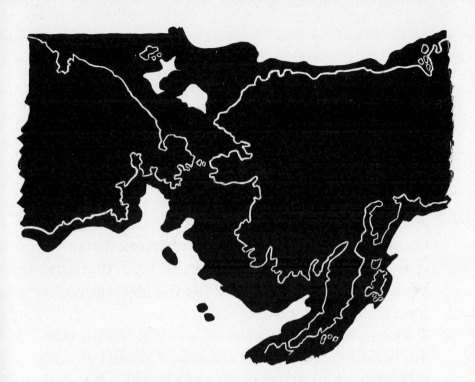

If the water level of the ocean was lowered 150 feet, the shore lines of Alaska and Siberia (outlined in white) would be spread into a broad band connecting the two continents (black area). The temperature and vegetation of this region as well as the shore line altered many times during the one million years of the great ice age

spring up. Grass and flowers grew. Even during the coldest part of the ice age, there were many starts and stops of glacier motion. Some of these pauses lasted for centuries before life-crushing movements began again.

A nomadic hunting band in a late ice-age landscape. Rounded, grass-covered hills were the home range of a vast population of big game animals ranging in size from the mammoth and giant bison to delicate antelope and deer

Similar signs of life are found today near the world's remaining glaciers, indicating that animals, plants, and men can live or at least travel at the very edges of glacial ice. Remains of thousands of frozen animals and plants have been collected from the thawing mucky soil of Asia and Alaska. Some specimens represent accidents; others were heaped together after death by the bulldozing action of moving ice.

[42]

More comparisons are needed to help scientists fully identify the distinctive mammals of the late ice age. Mammoths, mastodons, horses, camels, ground sloths, many types of deer, moose, caribou, several species of bison, large cats, and a wide variety of other big game are known to have lived from Florida to parts of Canada and Alaska. The same animals lived on the edge of salt marshes of the east coast to the La Brea tar pits of California. Such animals lived in North America in great numbers; their bones prove that. But when did they arrive, and when were they last seen on the land where their bones are found?

All of this is evidence that an abundance of animal and plant life once flourished on land which is barren and cold today. The jumble of soil and effects of erosion have prevented a clear understanding of climate changes and the soil layers of the ice age. The ice age was a time of rather sudden weather changes which brought torrential floods, landslides, and churning wet soil to hide the appearance of the land and signs of early man.

The answer to most of the puzzles concerning early Americans lies in what we hope to learn about the traveling habits of ancient hunting nomads. As

[43]

Mammoths were a major game animal for the prehistoric hunters of the late ice age. These grazing elephants migrated seasonally, following flat river bottoms and grassy ridges to reach their breeding or wintering territory

Ambushing a mastodon in wet and forested terrain

A mammoth was killed in many ways, but the safest pro-
cedure was to separate a young animal from the herd and
drive him into a trap. In addition to flint-tipped spears, the
hunters used small boulders, logs, and any other weapon that
would weaken the beast

yet, there are not enough sites of discovery to form a connected story of human migration during the ice age.

Vilhjalmur Stefansson, the famous scholar of the arctic, states that hunting Eskimos often traveled one thousand miles in a year in order to find the game necessary to survive. How this figure would apply to travel over more rugged and wooded landscape is unknown, but if such a walking range was possible, the spread of people through the two American continents might have been quite rapid.

Despite the known speed of ice-age events, a growing group of scholars has become convinced that earliest man reached North America *before,* rather than during or after, the last great advance of glacial ice. These men feel that our knowledge of ice-age man is too incomplete to permit us to think that all of his adjustments to his changing environment could have occurred in such a short time. If this theory proves to be correct, the first people of North America may have reached these shores one hundred thousand years ago.

Before exploring other facts which help date man on this continent, we should consider the theory that some hunters may have returned to Asia after

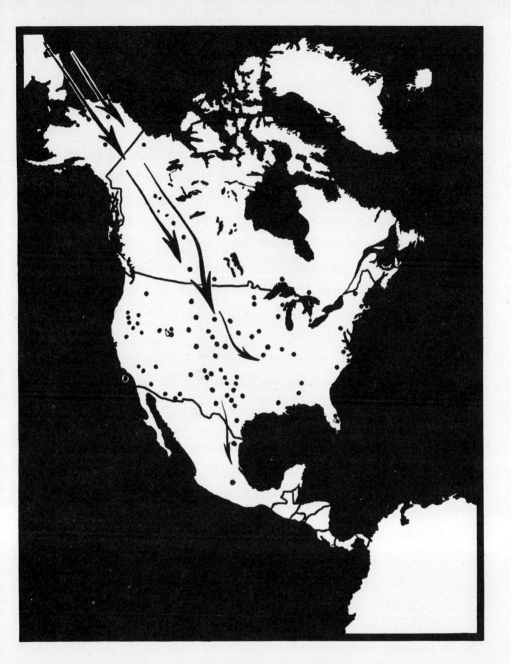

Routes of entry into North America used by primitive man.
(The more important sites of discovery are shown as dots.)
This concept of migration expresses the most popular view
held by archaeologists

living in North America. Support for this idea are spearheads, called Yuma points, whose shape and style of chipping is unique. The oldest Yuma points were discovered in Arizona. Later discoveries in Alaska and a similar spear point of a more recent date found near Lake Baikal in Russia suggest a route of travel into Asia from America.

The camel and the horse evolved in North America during many millions of years. During the ice age, both animals migrated to Asia where they have

Wild horses were common in many areas of North America before and during the ice age. Bones and teeth found at many sites show that early man hunted and ate this animal

*One of several varieties of camels
which once thrived in North America*

survived in a wild state until today. Some very
early American hunters may well have followed
these herds. The horse and camel prove that the
land bridge in the north contributed new species to
Asia and Europe just as it brought migrating people and other kinds of animals to these shores.

Anthropologists are unable to say how much this
two-way traffic influenced prehistoric America.

[49]

Since any bridge works in both directions, the actual events are confusing, and they will continue to be confusing until we explore the far north of both continents more completely.

Did primitive man become extinct as the animals became scarce? Did weather changes kill all of them? Did the growing human population kill too many of the slow-breeding big animals? The early men had fire; did they burn away the feeding range of the game herds? Did the early people drift east as the glaciers melted, or did they retreat north and over to Asia? Did any of the descendants of Folsom or Sandia hunt bison until Sitting Bull's day in the late nineteenth century?

It is tempting to compare the ancient bison and mammoth hunters to the familiar Plains Indians who hunted modern bison on horses stolen from the Spanish explorers. But there is no continuous record of such hunters to check. The earliest inhabitants of the great plains of America are poorly known from this standpoint.

To trace the evolution of men or animals, we must have a long series of discoveries representing one period of history after another. This kind of record exists for many animals, but heavy soil erosion in the western United States has hindered the

A blowout—wind-swept ground containing bones, flint chips, and other signs of early man. The steadily eroding surface leaves artifacts exposed on earth pedestals. The sun and abrasive action of the sand smooth and darken the surface of the objects

search there. Water and wind have revealed many treasures, but these same natural forces have scrambled or hidden other pieces of the puzzle.

In spite of yearly progress in the pursuit of the first Americans, today's digging teams still have almost the same hopes as did archaeologists in the 1920s. No one has found a complete human skeleton or even a skull in direct association with ancient flint points and prehistoric animal bones. Signs of an individual dwelling or a whole village are eagerly sought, burials are unknown, and there is no connected chain of sites which show man's route of entry into this continent.

There is some scattered skeletal material which is very old, but none is complete enough to help recreate a picture of the people. The few rare skull parts of ancient man are generally narrower than the skulls of more recent American Indians.

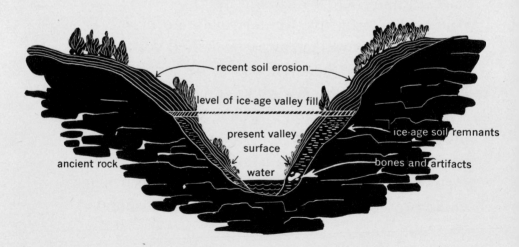

Exposure of artifacts by erosion

The scarcity of skeletons is not altogether unexpected, for bones of ancient people are very rare all over the world. Most of those which have been found come from caves or rock shelters where they had been well protected for centuries. Caves well suited to shelter human beings are scarce in the United States, and so there is not much to be learned from that source.

Another explanation for the scarcity of old human skeletons is the fact that few nomadic hunters anywhere in the world have ever buried their dead in the earth. Most primitive nomads placed their dead on platforms or in trees well out of reach of wolves and other scavengers. The more recent bison-hunting Plains Indians did this; perhaps the Paleo-Indians before them did it too.

Still other primitive hunters made no burials at all. They merely walked away from their dead companions, leaving their remains to be scattered by weather and the animals which trailed after them.

Almost the only remaining chance to recover significant old skeletons is from bones that have been preserved accidentally, in a landslide, a drowning, or a similar quick death under circumstances which would protect the body from weather and animals.

[53]

One of the most significant discoveries of this kind in the United States took place at Pelican Rapids, Minnesota, in 1931. The skeleton of a fifteen-year-old girl was found there in deep silt that had once been the bottom of an ice-age lake. A dagger made from elk antler, and a conch shell were found with the bones. Both had holes drilled in them, probably to be worn on a belt or looped over the shoulder.

The most important thing about the bones of this girl is that her long narrow skull and rather large teeth were typically primitive traits that anatomists have come to expect in ancient Americans. These same features have been noted in most of the other skulls of great age found in North America.

Such evidence is judged by men who are trained to recognize very small but important differences in skull structure. Comparing the rare old skulls of Paleo-Indians with those of more recent Indians, these scientists argue that the red-skinned people may not have been the descendants of the original Americans. Some anatomists favor the view that the early hunters resembled the dark-skinned primitive Australians; still others favor a brown-skinned Melanesian. But whatever the belief, most

A platform burial as practiced among Plains Indians of recent times. Wandering hunters in many parts of the world have used this or a similar burial form. The platform, wrappings, and stick framework protect the body until exposure ultimately destroys it

scholars agree that a people of well-mixed racial traits made the journey from Asia.

None of the many varieties of Indians on the two American continents resembles the typical Mongolian race of Asia. Eskimos are closest to this racial group and they are the most recent arrivals in North America. The majority of red-skinned peo-

[55]

ple are believed to have come as one of many groups that migrated to North America several thousand years ago, before the Eskimos, but thousands of years after the first hunters who followed the game herds from Asia.

These Indians were vigorous and culturally well advanced. They spread quickly over most of two large continents. In spite of some specialized evidence to the contrary, many people still prefer to believe that the Indians found by Columbus are the direct descendants of the people who lived at Sandia, Folsom, or the other sites where early man has been traced. But, since the human population of North America fifteen thousand or twenty thousand years ago was very small, it is not likely that all of the desired answers about early man will ever be found.

Today, we can not escape the feeling that science is on the verge of clearing up many details of man's past. More people are engaged in exploration, and many different scientific disciplines are working together to answer questions about early Americans that have puzzled men since the first Europeans encountered the Indians.

Since the perfection of carbon-14 dating methods, doubts about man's great age in the new world no longer exist. The greater problem now is to find sites which link together the events and show when and how the people of Asia first came to American shores.

In the meantime, discoveries are being made which may challenge Sandia man as the earliest inhabitant of this country and continent. Many years may pass before such explorations are complete and can be fully reported. For example, a site at Tule Springs, Nevada, was first discovered in 1933, and it has been in the news until the present time. Some of the early discoveries made there resulted in a tentative date of approximately twenty-three thousand years for the site. More recent explorations brought forward additional hearths and the bones of camel, bison, mammoths, and horses

Major sites of discovery in the western United States. These sites relate to variations of flint-chipping styles that have produced distinctive spear points

which had been cooked and eaten there. Premature publicity about these finds reported that a new radiocarbon date of thirty-two thousand years had been assigned to charcoal from that location. This date did not prove to be valid, and the men in charge of the project withdrew all comment on the age of the site.

For the same reason, many important materials have lain in museum cabinets for ten to twenty years without being reported publicly. These specimens are awaiting the eventual discovery of comparable relics of man, or the animals he hunted, which can be accurately dated.

All of this means that there are numerous contenders for the uneasy crown of antiquity worn today by Sandia man. Leading candidates are known from Nebraska, Montana, Nevada, Arizona, Texas, Mexico, and many other places. The new name for the oldest-known Americans may be linked to work at Clovis, Pinto Basin, Silver Lake, Tule Springs, Hell Gap, Mohave, or derived from any one of a dozen obscure sites too small to appear on a map.

But all of these names, as well as that of Sandia man himself, belong to a faceless people. No skull or complete skeleton of a Paleo-Indian hunter ex-

[58]

ists, at least none which can be undeniably linked with old tools or flint points and the bones of extinct animals.

There is little doubt that a "new" earliest American will be described someday soon. At the moment, the elusive big game hunter who rates that honor is named for the Sandia Mountains of New Mexico, and he is recognized by a few things that can be held in the palm of a man's hand:

A distinctive flint spear point.
Some scraps of charcoal.
The teeth and scraps of bone from an animal that has been extinct for more than 25,000 years.

This is all that we have to identify the earliest American.

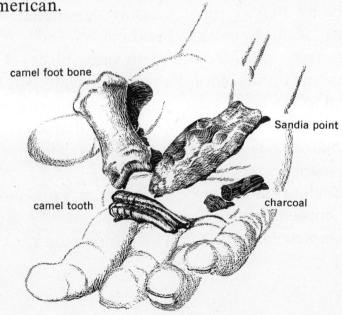

camel foot bone

Sandia point

camel tooth

charcoal

ABOUT THE AUTHOR

WILLIAM E. SCHEELE, Director of the Natural Science Museum of Cleveland, was born in that city in 1920. He won scholarships in art and biology and was graduated from Western Reserve University in 1947. In November, 1939, he won the first annual Bird Art Contest sponsored by the then Cleveland Museum of Natural History, and the next day he was a member of their staff. In 1949, after army service had interrupted his career, he was appointed director of the museum. Mr. Scheele's outside activities include painting natural-history subjects (he has exhibited in many museums) and fossil hunting. He lives with his wife and three sons on a tree farm near Chardon, Ohio. He is the author of several books for young people, including most recently *The Mound Builders* and *The Cave Hunters* and, for older boys and girls, *Prehistoric Man and the Primates.*